D1332154

Nelson

ENGLISH

SKILLS

BOOK 1

JOHN JACKMAN
WENDY WREN

Nelson

Contents

Vocabulary	Punctuation/ Grammar	Spelling	Quiz
big bigger biggest	a or an (vowels, consonants)	alphabetical order ee and ea	hidden words
compound words of and off	sentences nouns	magic 'e'	alphabetical order codes
homophones	singular and plural nouns, adjectives	ow ar	alphabetical order cartoon faces
order words	verbs	dictionary work sh	punctuation puzzle word families
was and were	colours as adjectives colours as nouns	wa	sentence machine
definitions onomatopoeia	sentences verbs	ea+r	ou pattern
contractions (apostrophe)	addresses	oo	odd-one-out
dictionary work	question mark conjunctions	ck	hidden words
Latin words	commas	soft 'c'	punctuation puzzle crossword
days and months	proper nouns	th	letter squares

Bees

A drone and
some worker bees

Three kinds of bees live in this hive.
Most of the bees are small worker bees.
A few are a little bigger.
These are the male bees, called drones.

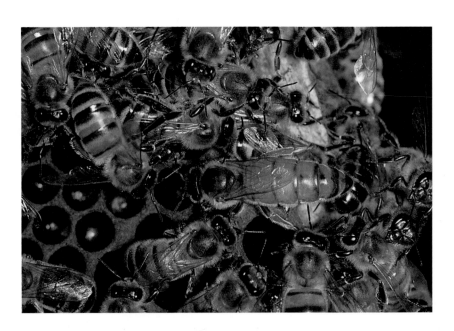

The queen and
some worker bees

The biggest bee is the queen.
The queen stays in the hive.
She does not go out to find food.
She lays eggs all the time.
The worker bees feed her.

Christine Butterworth

COMPREHENSION

A Copy these sentences. Fill in the missing words.

1 There are ＿＿ kinds of bees in a hive.

2 Male bees are called ＿＿.

3 The smallest bees are the ＿＿ bees.

B Write a sentence to answer each question.

1 Where do the bees live?

2 Which is the biggest bee in the hive?

3 Why do the worker bees need to feed the queen bee?

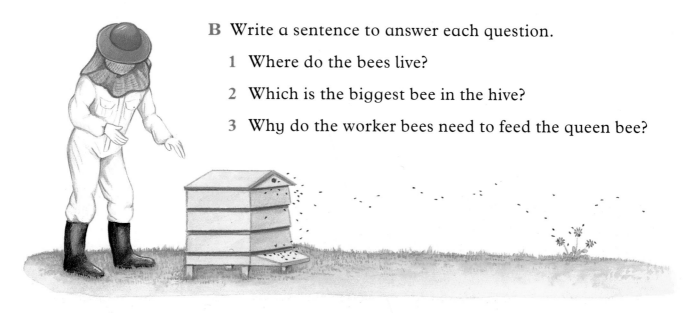

VOCABULARY

big bigger biggest

Something is **bigger** or **smaller** than *one* other thing.
Something is the **biggest** or the **smallest** of *three or more* things.

worker bee

A Copy these sentences. Fill in the missing words.

1 Workers are s＿＿ bees.

2 The queen is a b＿＿ bee.

3 A drone is b＿＿ than a worker bee.

4 A worker bee is s＿＿ than a drone.

5 Drones are s＿＿ than the queen.

6 The queen is the b＿＿ bee in the hive.

queen bee

B Write a few sentences about your family using some of these words.

drone

| big | bigger | biggest |
| small | smaller | smallest |

5

Here are the 26 letters in the alphabet.

a b c d e f g h i j k l m n o p q r s t u v w x y z

A 1 What is the first letter?

2 What is the last letter?

3 Which letter comes after **o**?

4 Which letter comes after **t**?

5 Which letter comes before **l**?

6 Which letter comes before **f**?

7 Does **m** come before or after **n**?

8 Does **t** come before or after **s**?

Vowel letters

> These five letters are special. They are called **vowels**.
> a e i o u
> There is a **vowel** or a letter **y** in every word.

A Copy ten words from this page and draw a neat circle round the vowel letter(s) in each word.

'ee' and 'ea' pattern

A 1 Draw or cut out five bee shapes. Write an **ee** word on each bee.

2 Draw a large leaf. Find as many **ea** words as you can to write on the leaf.

B Choose an **ee** or **ea** word to finish each sentence.

1 The ____ stung my leg.

2 The ____ had pink blossom.

3 I like to ____ honey.

4 The ____ bee lays all the eggs.

leaf

bee

Remember
the vowels are
a e i o u.

Use **an** before words that begin with a vowel.
You can hear that this makes them easier to say.
  Examples: **an** ant, **an** egg
Use **a** before words that begin with any other letter.
Letters that are not vowels are called **consonants**.
  Examples: **a** bee, **a** drone

A Write **a** or **an** before each of these words.

1 _____ flower   2 _____ queen   3 _____ egg

4 _____ orange   5 _____ ant   6 _____ petal

7 _____ hive   8 _____ bee   9 _____ apple

B Make a list of some more words that would need
to have **an** in front of them.

Find a small word hidden in each of these words.
Sometimes there is more than one hidden word!

1 worker	2 bigger	3 little	4 been
5 alphabet	6 honey	7 drone	8 letter

Earthworms

When you dig in the garden you can often see an earthworm. Pick it up gently. It won't hurt you.

Its body is made of many rings, or segments. If a worm's tail gets cut off it might not die. The bigger part can grow a new tail.

An earthworm has no eyes, but it knows when it is day and when it is night. When it senses daylight it will move back underground.

An earthworm first digs a long burrow. Then it makes smaller tunnels. This mixes the soil which helps the plants to grow. Worms eat dead plants and soil as they crawl along their burrows.

After rain you may see earthworms on top of the ground. Rainwater can fill their burrows, so they come to the surface to breathe.

COMPREHENSION

A Copy these sentences. Fill in the missing words.

1 Earthworms will not ____ you if you pick them up.

2 An earthworm has no ____.

3 Worms make long ____.

B Write a sentence to answer each question.

1 Where do earthworms live?

2 Do earthworms always die if they are cut in two?

3 What do worms eat?

4 If you were a worm what would you fear most?

Compound words are made by joining two words.
Example: earth + worm = **earthworm**

A Find four different compound words in the passage about earthworms. Here are some clues:

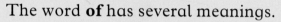

under	earth	water	light
worm	rain	ground	day

B Find some more compound words in your reading book.

of and off

The word **of** has several meanings.
Examples: The worm came out **of** the soil.
Its body is made **of** equal parts.
The word **off** usually means the opposite of 'on'.
Never use **off** and **of** next to each other.
Examples: The worm crawled **off** her hand.
The worm crawled **off of** her hand.

A Copy these sentences putting **of** or **off** in the gaps.

1 Six ____ us went digging for worms.

2 I was careful not to cut ____ the end of the worm.

3 We took ____ our dirty boots.

4 The worm's body is made ____ segments.

B Write about this picture. Put **off** or **of** in each sentence.

Sentences begin with a **capital letter** and end with a **full stop**.

A Write these sentences. Begin each one with a capital letter and end it with a full stop.

1 we dug the soil in the garden

2 we found lots of earthworms

3 our teacher helped us make a wormery

4 worms like damp soil but it must not be too wet

5 worms eat dead plants

A **noun** is the name of something.
Examples: earthworm, garden, rain, soil.

Nouns are sometimes called 'naming' words.

A Copy these words and put a tick by the nouns.

| is | leaf | hot | earth |
| bigger | stone | dug | garden |

B Copy these sentences. Fill in the missing nouns.

1 Some ____ like to eat ____.

2 The ____ dug her garden with a ____.

3 The ____ does not like ____ in its burrow.

10

The magic 'e' at the end of a word usually makes the vowel sound like its own name.
Example: b**i**t + e = b**i**te

A Copy these words. Then add an **e** and write them again.

1 hid   2 rid   3 tap   4 pip   5 hop   6 us

What has happened to the sound of each vowel letter?

B Find five more words which have a magic 'e'.

> Here are the 26 letters of the alphabet.
> A B C D E F G H I J K L M N O P Q R S T U V W X Y Z

Copy these sentences. Fill in the missing letters.

1 The letter ____ comes after the letter **D**.

2 The letter **R** comes after the letter ____.

3 The letter ____ comes before **W**.

4 The letter ____ comes before **P**.

5 The letter **Y** comes after the letter ____.

6 The letter ____ comes between **M** and **O**.

Codes

Look at this code.

> A B C D E F G H I J K L M N O P Q R S T U V W X Y Z
> 1 2 3 4 5 6 7 8 9 10 11 12 13 14 15 16 17 18 19 20 21 22 23 24 25 26

1 Here are some words written in the code.
Crack the code and write the words.

23 15 18 13   18 15 23   7 1 18 4 5 14   3 18 1 23 12

2 Write this sentence in code: **The worm digs a burrow.**

3 Make some code words for a friend to crack.

Springtime on the farm

Newborn

Down behind the thistles,
In the gully, near the creek,
Lies something wet and shining,
Something very weak.
Its legs are rather wobbly,
It's very, very shy,
It's nuzzling for its first meal,
Though it's not yet dry.
It's got a velvet nose,
But a rough little tongue.
It's a newborn calf,
With its proud cow-mum.

Gayle Sweeney

COMPREHENSION

A Copy these sentences. Fill in the missing words.

1 The calf was born near the ____.

2 Its nose feels like ____.

3 Its ____ are rather wobbly.

B Write a sentence to answer each question.

1 Which words describe the young calf's tongue?

2 How does the cow feel about her new calf?

3 Why do farmers often keep animals in fields next to a river or creek?

These three words have the **same** sound.

    to   two   too

They have **different** meanings and spellings.

Words like these are called **homophones**.

Two farmers **too** tired **to** work.

A Write sentences using these words.

1 two cats   2 to the farm   3 ten to two

4 too tall   5 too big   6 two bulls

B Find the homophones in the poem to match these words.

1 week   2 inn   3 creak   4 knows   5 ruff

Write them side by side. Like this: **1** week weak

When we talk about only one thing it is **singular**.

When we talk about two or more things they are **plural**.

singular		plural
cow	+ s =	cows
leg	+ s =	legs

A What is the plural of these words?

1 tractor   2 dog   3 plant   4 farmer

5 thistle   6 field   7 boy   8 girl

Adjectives

Adjectives are sometimes called 'describing' words.

Adjectives tell us more about nouns.
They make our writing much more interesting.
Examples:

adjective noun	**adjective** noun	**adjective** noun
angry farmer	**black** cat	**fierce** bull

A Choose the adjective from the box which best describes each noun in these pictures.

dirty	muddy	red	angry	long
fierce	brown	thin	enormous	
ugly	strong	green	frightened	loud

1
2
3
4
5
6

B Copy one of the pictures or draw your own.
Write some adjectives to describe it. Like this:

young, bouncy, soft, pretty,
brown, naughty, mischievous

C Write at least ten adjectives to describe this picture.

'ow' pattern
crow

cow

A Read these words. Listen to their sounds.

row	owl	slow	know	crowd
bow	yellow	flower	own	down
town	flow	now	snow	blow

Write two headings like this:
cow   crow
Sort the words in the box into their sound groups.
Some words might go under both headings.

'ar' pattern

A This sentence has lots of **ar** sounds in it:

The farmer parked her large car in the farmyard by the barn.

1 Write a list of as many words as you can which have the **ar** sound as in 'farm'.

2 Make your own sentence with lots of **ar** words in it.

QUIZ

Alphabetical order

A B C D E F G H I J K L M N O P Q R S T U V W X Y Z
Write each group of letters in alphabetical order.

1 T I F R   2 A N E D J   3 P W S H L Y

4 F D B A C E G   5 The letters of your first name.

Cartoon faces

Think of an adjective to describe each of these faces.

1   2   3

Snowy weather

The snow has blown
Against our door
And the radio says
There'll be lots more.

Snow is exciting. It makes everywhere look pretty and it is good fun to play in.

Snow is made when the air is very cold. Delicate crystals of ice form in the clouds. Each snowflake is a crystal that grows in a repeating pattern. Can you see the patterns in this picture? As the crystals touch each other they stick together. Then they gently flutter to the ground.

Snow settles on trees and can sometimes break off branches with its weight. On the roads it can bring danger. It can make it difficult for farmers to feed their animals.

If there is a snowstorm, and the snow gets very deep, it can even make it impossible for some children to get to school!

A Copy these sentences. Fill in the missing words.

1 Snow is made when the air is very ____.

2 Thick snow can break ____ off trees.

3 The snow is very deep after a ____.

B Write a sentence to answer each question.

1 What happens when the snow crystals touch each other?

2 Why do farmers not like the snow?

3 What do you not like about snowy days?

VOCABULARY

Order words

> The **first** season in the year is Winter, Spring is **second**, Summer is **third** and Autumn is **fourth**.

A Copy these sentences. Fill in the gaps with an order word.

1 Winter is the ____ season in the year.

2 The ____ season each year is Autumn.

3 Summer is the ____ season.

4 The ____ season is Spring.

B Answer the questions about this sledge race.
These words will help you: first, second, third, fourth, fifth, sixth, seventh, eighth, ninth, tenth.

1 Who is first?

2 What is Jane's position?

3 What is Lee's position?

4 Who is tenth?

5 Who is last?

6 How is Azra doing?

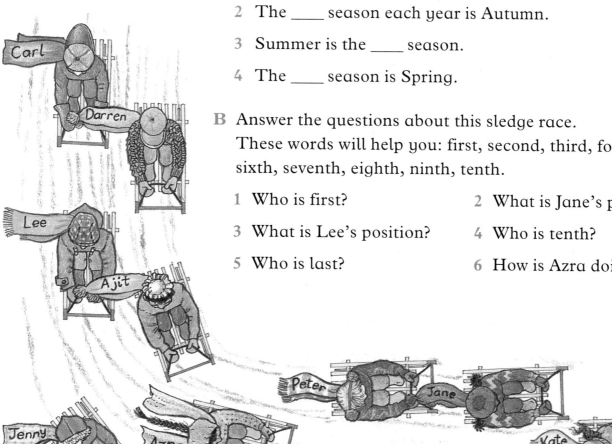

17

GRAMMAR

Verbs

Verbs are sometimes called 'doing' words.

> A **verb** is an active word.
> It tells us what is being done in a sentence.
> *Example:* The wind **blows** the snow.

A Use the verbs in the box to make these word webs.
Choose verbs which go with each noun.
Draw the webs.

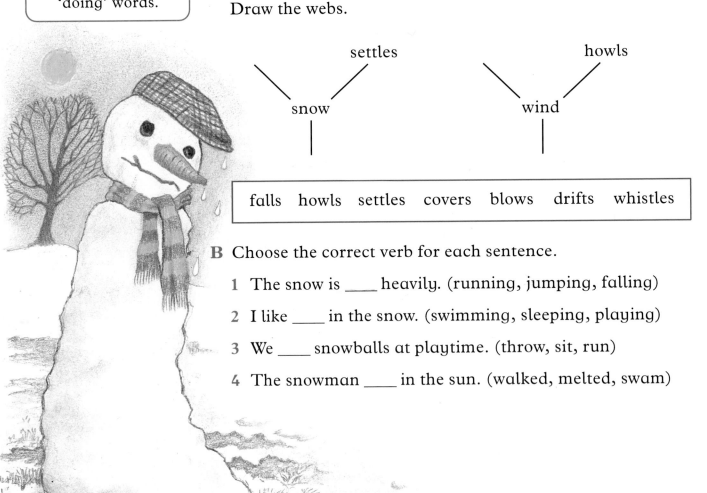

settles   howls

snow   wind

| falls howls settles covers blows drifts whistles |

B Choose the correct verb for each sentence.

1 The snow is ____ heavily. (running, jumping, falling)

2 I like ____ in the snow. (swimming, sleeping, playing)

3 We ____ snowballs at playtime. (throw, sit, run)

4 The snowman ____ in the sun. (walked, melted, swam)

SPELLING

Vowel order

Don't be shy, have a try!

A 1 What are the five vowel letters?
(Look back to page 6 if you can't remember.)

2 Which is the first vowel?

3 Which is the last vowel?

4 Which is the middle vowel?

5 Write a word which does not have a vowel.
(Which letter in your word sounds like a vowel?)

18

Dictionary work

> Words in a dictionary are in alphabetical order.
> Words starting with **a** come first, words starting with **b** come second, words starting with **c** come third, and so on to words starting with **z**. These are last.

A Can you put these lists of words in alphabetical order? The first one is done to help you.

a b c d e f g h i j k l m n o p q r s t u v w x y z

1 Spring, Autumn, Winter = Autumn, Spring, Winter

2 snow, frost, ice

3 wind, blizzard, drift

4 rain, hail, sleet

'sh' pattern

> We say **sh** if we want someone to be quiet.
> It is also an important letter pattern.

A 1 Write ten words that begin with **sh**.
Like this: **sh**ort **sh**arp **sh**owers

2 Write ten words that have **sh** in the middle or at the end. Like this: spla**sh**, wa**sh**, wi**sh**ing

QUIZ
Punctuation puzzle

Write these sentences correctly. You will need to put in the word spaces. Don't forget the capital letters and full stops.

1 thesnowiscoldandwet

2 ilikethrowingsnowballs

3 thesnowmanismeltinginthesun

Word families

Each of these word families needs four words.
Can you find one more in the brackets?

1 Spring, Summer, Autumn (snow, Winter, windy)

2 wind, snow, frost (sweets, rain, bus)

3 cold, hot, freezing (dinner, warm, red)

Check-up 1

VOCABULARY

A Write the missing words.
The words in the brackets will help you.

1 Gina the clown is ____ than her sisters.
   (small, smaller, smallest)

2 She rode the ____ bicycle. (big, bigger, biggest)

3 Gina fell ____ the bicycle. (of, off)

4 She landed in a tub ____ jelly. (of, off)

5 Her sisters' shoes were ____ big for them. (to, too, two)

6 Gina found it hard ____ ride her bicycle. (to, too, two)

7 Her ____ sisters had to lift her up. (to, too, two)

GRAMMAR AND
PUNCTUATION

A Write **a** or **an** before each of these words.

1 ____ prize   2 ____ ice-cream

3 ____ apple   4 ____ balloon

B Write these sentences, putting in the capital letters
and full stops.

1 we had great fun at the circus

2 i liked the tightrope walker

C Read this sentence carefully.

The clever juggler caught the red ball.

Now answer these questions about it.

1 Write the two nouns ('naming' words).

2 Which word is a verb ('active' word)?

3 Write the two adjectives ('describing' words).

D Write the plural of each noun.

1 girl   2 boy   3 acrobat

4 juggler   5 clown   6 dancer

> Remember, **plural** means more than one.

SPELLING   A Answer these questions about the alphabet.

abcdefghijklmnopqrstuvwxyz

1 Which letter comes after **f**?

2 Which letter follows **p**?

3 Does **c** come before or after **d**?

4 Does **v** come after **u**?

5 Which letter comes between **h** and **j**?

6 Which of these letters are vowels?
   a b c d e

7 Which letters are missing?
   p q _ _ _ u v w

8 Write these letters in alphabetical order.
   j t d a o

9 Write these words in alphabetical order.
   clown ball act drop

10 Write these words in alphabetical order.
   people circus ticket fun

Looking at colours

Most light comes from the sun. The sun's rays can make many different colours as they shine through dust and tiny water droplets high in the sky. On a bright sunny day the sky looks blue. As the sun rises or sets on a clear day the sky fills with other beautiful colours – gold, red, orange and violet.

When rays of sunlight shine through rain, or spray from a waterfall, we can see even more lovely colours. These are the colours of the rainbow.

COMPREHENSION

A Copy these sentences. Fill in the missing words.

1 Most light comes from the _Sun_ .

2 On a sunny day the sky looks _blue_

3 When the sun shines through rain it makes a ____ .

B Write a sentence to answer each question.

1 What colours might you see in the sky at sunset?

2 Why does the sky fill with beautiful colours?

3 Why don't we see a beautiful sunset every day?

Was is used for one person or thing.
Example: Gemma **was** watching the sunset.

Were is used for more than one person or thing.
Example: Craig and Ajay **were** watching the sunset.

Were is also used with **you**, whether it is one or more than one person.
Example: I saw **you were** watching the sunset.

A Write these sentences putting **was** or **were** in the gaps.

1 The sun ____ shining as I ____ walking home.

2 My friends ____ walking in front of me.

3 We ____ all surprised when it started to rain.

4 The rainbow ____ fantastic.

5 "You____ lucky to see that," said Mum.

The colours of the rainbow are:

Red	Can you see that the first letters
Orange	spell out a man's name?
Yellow	
Green	**ROY G BIV**
Blue	
Indigo	This will help you to remember the
Violet	colours of the rainbow.

A Use a rainbow colour to describe these foods.

1 a ____ banana   2 a ____ cherry   3 a ____ beetroot

4 a ____ cabbage   5 ____ cheese   6 an ____ carrot

B Look at this puzzle.
Find six colours and write them down.
You can go down or across.
One is done to help you.

```
k   u   t   f   y   e
n   g   r   e   e   n
p   u   r   p   l   e
i   s   e   k   l   v
n   z   d   g   o   i
k   b   r   o   w   n
```

Colours as nouns

What is yellow? Pears are yellow,
Rich and ripe and mellow.
What is green? The grass is green,
With small flowers in between.
What is violet? Clouds are violet
In the summer twilight.
What is orange? Why an orange,
Just an orange.

Christina Rossetti

A In this poem most of the colours are adjectives
describing something.
Can you see one colour word which is a thing – **a noun**?

B

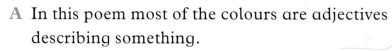

orange	bright	striped	violet
pale	green	lemon	spotted

Look at the words above. Write each sentence and fill in
the gap with a noun which can also be a colour.

1 The children played on the village ____ .

2 I like ____ with my pancakes.

3 My favourite flower is a ____ .

4 An ____ is my favourite fruit.

Look
Cover
Remember
Write
Check

The words in the box are worth learning.
The **a** sounds like the **o** in 'h**o**t' and can catch us out if we aren't careful.
Write these words and try to remember them.
Ask a friend to test you.

was	**wa**sh	s**wa**n
wasp	**wa**tch	s**wa**mp
want	**wa**nd	s**wa**llow

A Write a word from the box to answer these riddles.

1 We should do this before we eat our meals.

2 An insect which can sting.

3 A large, white bird.

4 You wear this on your wrist.

5 A little word found in 'wasp' and 'wash'.

QUIZ

Sentence machine

Take one word or phrase from each box to make a sensible sentence. Write it down.

The wasp Our baby My dog	chased stung threw	the rattle the cat the swan	under in on	the custard. its neck. the shed.

Now make some silly sentences.
It is more fun to make nonsense sentences.
Draw a picture of your funniest one.

25

Ears

We hear sounds through our ears. Our ears collect sound. If you cup your hand round your ear you can collect more sound. Try to make a funnel with a piece of paper. Can you collect even more sound?

Our ears are delicate. We must always be careful not to put anything in them or we may damage them forever.

Sounds come into our outer ear.

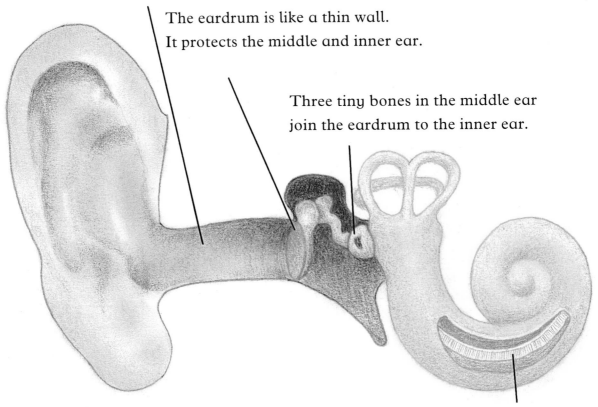

The eardrum is like a thin wall. It protects the middle and inner ear.

Three tiny bones in the middle ear join the eardrum to the inner ear.

The inner ear is a tiny tube filled with liquid and tiny hairs.

Sounds make the eardrum move, or vibrate, which makes the bones in the middle ear vibrate, which makes the hairs in the inner ear vibrate. The brain can tell what kind of sound is heard by the way these hairs move.

A Copy these sentences. Fill in the missing words.

1 We hear through our ____ .

2 The eardrum is like a thin ____ .

3 ____ make the eardrum vibrate.

B Write a sentence to answer each question.

1 How can we collect more sound for our ear?

2 What does the eardrum protect?

3 Why should we never put anything in our ears?

VOCABULARY

Definitions

The **definition** of a word tells us what it means.

A These words and definitions have been mixed up.
Write the correct definition next to each word.

protect	easily damaged
tiny	tube with a wide mouth
damage	keep safe
funnel	very small
delicate	shake
vibrate	harm

B Now write your own definition of 'ear'.
Check your definition with the definition in a dictionary.

Onomatopoeia

(On-oh-mat-oh-pee-a)

That's a long word.
I just call them
'sound' words.

Sometimes we make words from the sound they describe.
These 'sound' words are called **onomatopoeic** words.
Examples: The stone went **plop** in the water.
       I heard the **hiss** of the snake.

A Choose an onomatopoeic word from the box below
to match each sound.

clank	rumble	splash
crackle	crunch	creak

1 walking on dry leaves   2 distant thunder

3 burning twigs   4 opening a rusty gate

5 jumping into water   6 dropping a heavy chain

GRAMMAR

Sentences

Remember,
the verb is
the 'active' or
'doing' word.

Every sentence must make sense. There are three things a
sentence needs to help it make sense:
a **capital letter**, a **verb** and a **full stop**.

A Write these sentences, putting in the capital letter and
full stop. Underline the verb. The first one is done for you.

1 peter hurt his ear
   Peter <u>hurt</u> his ear.

2 she heard the noise

3 the teacher clapped her hands

4 i saw lightning

B Write two sentences of your own about sounds.

Look
Cover
Remember
Write
Check

A These words have the **ea + r** pattern and rhyme with 'ear'.

year	hear	dear	fear	near	rear

Choose a word from the box above to match each definition.

1 at the back
2 someone loved
3 to be afraid
4 twelve months
5 close by
6 to listen to

Write down all the **ou** words you can find in this picture.

Chinese penfriend

Dear Kim,

Hello. My name is Wong Chu Yin. My family name comes first, so my friends call me Chu Yin. I live in China.

I'm writing to tell you about myself and my family. I'm sending you some photos. I hope you'll write back and tell me about yourself.

I live in a big village. Most people in China live in villages. My parents are farmers.

I sometimes go to see my cousins who live in the noisy city. My aunt is a doctor and my uncle works in a factory that makes television sets. I like visiting them but I always like to come home.

In our village we grow rice, but we also grow vegetables and keep pigs, chickens and ducks. The rice grows in fields that we flood with water. These fields are called 'paddies', and are like small ponds. Water buffalo, which are very strong and like the water, plough the paddies. We wade through the water planting rice seedlings. This is fun at first, but I sometimes get cold!

Most people in our village go to work on bicycles. We carry loads to and from the fields in baskets on bamboo poles on our shoulders. We sell about half the food we grow at the market so that we'll have money to buy clothes and meat. The other half we eat ourselves.

Please write and tell me all about you and your family and where you live.

Best wishes,

Chu Yin

A Copy these sentences. Fill in the missing words.

1 Chu Yin lives in ____.

2 Chu Yin's parents grow ____ and ____ .

3 Planting rice sometimes makes Chu Yin feel ____.

B Write a sentence to answer each question.

1 What animals are kept in Chu Yin's village?

2 How is rice grown?

3 Why do you think Chu Yin prefers to live in the country?

> When we speak we sometimes run words together.
> When we write these words we put an apostrophe (')
> to show letters have been left out.
> These are called **contractions**.
> *Examples:*   **I'm** = I am
>   **don't** = do not

A Look at Chu Yin's letter. Copy out the contractions.
You should be able to find three different ones.

B Write down these two lists, but match the words correctly.
The first is done for you.

it's = it is

it's	should not
shouldn't	let us
can't	it is
didn't	cannot
let's	did not

C Write these contractions in full. The first is done for you.

1 I'm = I am   2 you'll   3 doesn't   4 we'll

5 haven't   6 they're   7 weren't   8 she's

31

D Copy this passage but put contractions for the underlined words.

There is a party today. Chu Yin's cousins <u>cannot</u> come as <u>they are</u> too far away. <u>That is</u> a pity because <u>we will</u> have lots of food and fun.

PUNCTUATION

Addresses

We write addresses on envelopes.

A Write a sentence to answer each question.

1 Why do we write addresses on envelopes?

2 Why is it important that we write addresses clearly?

B When we write the name of the town on an envelope it should all be in capital letters.

1 Draw a rectangle about the size of an envelope. Copy this name and address.

> Sarah Richards
> 3 Grass Hill
> MORETON
> Somerset
> TN7 8QT

2 Now pretend you are writing a letter to a friend or a relative.
Write his or her name and address in the same way.

A Read these words.

bamboo   flood   door   foot

Can you hear how the **oo** letters make a different sound in each word?

There are many words which have **oo** in them. Find as many as you can and sort them into their sound groups. This picture will help you.

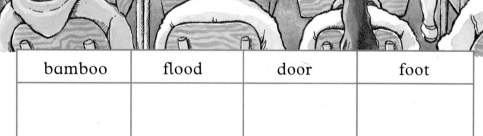

bamboo	flood	door	foot

Copy out each group of words.
Put a ring round the odd one out in each group.

1 horse cow pig crocodile sheep

2 bus car coach bicycle lorry

3 rice peas potatoes cabbage water

4 house aeroplane nest hutch burrow

5 China Scotland France Wales Birmingham

Rubbish in our community

We say that something is rubbish if we throw it away because we don't want it.

Rubbish can be:

sweet papers	food
crisp packets	old newspapers
empty tins and cans	dead flowers
cardboard boxes	glass and plastic bottles
	. . . and lots more!

If all the drink cans that people in the world used last year were put end to end, they would probably reach to the moon!

34

Every day each person in Britain throws away more than half a kilogram of rubbish. That is about:

4·5 kilograms of rubbish
in a week

18 kilograms of rubbish
in a month

216 kilograms of rubbish
in a year

A family of four people throws away about 750 kilograms of rubbish in a year.

Gervase Phinn

COMPREHENSION

A Copy these sentences. Fill in the missing words.

1 The things we throw away we call ____ .

2 Every day each of us throws away more than ____ a kilogram of rubbish.

3 The rubbish one person throws away each year weighs about as much as a ____ .

B Write a sentence to answer each question.

1 Name three types of rubbish you have thrown away this week.

2 What sorts of rubbish might be used again?

3 Why can it be dangerous to go on to rubbish tips?

Words in a dictionary are in alphabetical order.

A Put each of these lists of words in alphabetical order. This means you put them in the order in which their first letters come in the alphabet.
The first is done to help you.

abcdefghijklmnopqrstuvwxyz
1st   2nd   3rd

1 litter, tins, ash

Answer: ash, **litter**, tins
        1st   2nd   3rd

2 card, paper, box

3 plastic, can, bottle

4 rubbish, broken, tip, peelings

5 food, crisps, glass, metal

When we write a sentence which is a question we put a **question mark** (?) at the end.

Example: Why is there so much rubbish**?**

We don't need a full stop as well because the question mark already has one.

A Copy these sentences putting in the capital letters and question marks.

1 will you help me empty the dustbin

2 how many cans did they collect

3 why are so many useful things thrown away

4 how do we know that so many cans are thrown away

5 can we find ways to use them again

Conjunctions are sometimes called 'joining' words.

Conjunctions are words which are used to join two sentences. The two conjunctions we use most are:

and   but

Examples:

Take the rubbish outside. Put it in the dustbin.

Take the rubbish outside **and** put it in the dustbin.

That bin is heavy. This bin is light.

That bin is heavy **but** this bin is light.

We often use **but** if the sentences have opposite meanings.

A Write these sentences using **and** or **but** to join them.

1 We collected the rubbish. We threw it all away.

2 Some rubbish is buried. Some rubbish is burned.

3 We wanted a jumble sale. There was not much to sell.

4 We saved our newspapers. They were recycled.

SPELLING

'ck' pattern

| duck | truck | sack | crack | pack | packet |
| neck | wreck | stick | kick | chicken | rock | sock |

A Write down the **ck** words which are in the box and which are also in the picture.

QUIZ

Hidden words

Find one small word hidden in each of these words.
Write the big word and the small word next to each other.

dustbin plastic sort rubbish throw paper community

Roman sports

Chariot racing was one of the most popular activities in Roman times.

Thousands of people would go to watch the races. The biggest stadium was the Circus Maximus. This held 250,000 people. This means it was about three times as big as our biggest football stadiums.

There were four famous chariot racing clubs in Rome. Each club had different colours. There were up to 24 races a day.

The best charioteers, who were often slaves, became rich and famous. But chariot racing was very dangerous and often racers and their horses were killed.

Between the races the Romans watched gladiators fight to the death. Not all of the entertainment was so blood-thirsty. There were also acrobats, clowns and jugglers to watch.

COMPREHENSION

A Copy these sentences. Fill in the missing words.

1 In Roman times chariot ____ was very popular.

2 The biggest stadium was the ____ ____ .

3 There were ____ famous chariot racing clubs.

B Write a sentence to answer each question.

1 How many races were held each day?

2 What else was there to see at the stadium?

3 What was the worst thing about being a charioteer?

Most Romans spoke Latin. Many words we still use today were first brought here by the Romans.

A Copy the Latin words below.
Next to each one write what you think it means.
The answers are jumbled up in the box.

circus	familia
tuba	secundus
villa	medicus
actor	aqua

family	actor	house	long trumpet
circus	second	water	doctor

B **1** Which of our months was named after the Roman emperor Julius Caesar?

2 Which of our months was named after Emperor Augustus?

We use a **comma** (,) to separate each word in a list.

Example: The Romans liked to watch chariots, gladiators, jugglers, clowns and acrobats.

Do you see that instead of a comma we put **and** between the last two things in the list?

A Write these sentences. Put in the missing commas.

1 The Romans conquered England Wales and France.

2 Wheat barley rye oats and rice were all grown in the Roman Empire.

3 In the Roman town of Ostia there were painters bakers ferrymen clerks and messengers.

4 Roman gods included Juno Mars Venus and Mercury.

What do you notice about 'circus'?

The letter **c** is usually a sound like '**c** for **c**at'.
Sometimes it is soft, and sounds like **s**.
Say these words to yourself.

race   face   citizen   circus   fierce   France

A 1 Write out the words in the box.
Put a neat circle round the 'soft' **c** in each word.

2 Now underline the letter in each word which comes after the 'soft' **c**. Do you notice anything interesting?

3 Write some more words with 'soft' **c**.
Use a book to help you.

Remember, all the names have capital letters.

All the capital letters, full stops, question marks, apostrophes and commas have been left out of this piece of writing.
Copy it out neatly, putting in all the missing punctuation.

i dont think i would have liked to be a roman soldier they were sent away to cold places like belgium france holland and england sometimes they had to fight fierce battles im sure i would not have liked it arent you

Which words about Rome would answer this puzzle?

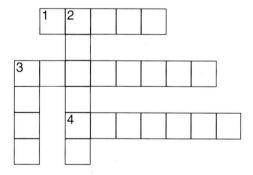

Words going across

1 The Roman language. (5 letters)
3 They performed between chariot races. (8 letters)
4 Circus Maximus was one. (7 letters)

Words going down

2 Month named after a Roman emperor. (6 letters)
3 Another month named after an emperor. (4 letters)

Anglo-Saxons

Many villages were first started by the Anglo-Saxons. Often they built their houses close together round a village green. Sometimes they would make a fence round the village to keep out wild animals and their enemies.

The village leader was called the thane. One of the biggest buildings was the thane's hall. This was like a large barn and had a thatched roof. The villagers met there for feasts. Most Anglo-Saxon churches were made of wood, but a few stone ones are still standing today.

Most villages had a miller, a blacksmith and a carpenter. In some villages there would also be a weaver, a potter and a tanner. So the Anglo-Saxons could find most things they needed for their simple lives in their village.

The Anglo-Saxons made their clothes of wool and dyed them simple, bright colours. The women wore long dresses, called tunics. The men wore trousers and short tunics.

COMPREHENSION

A Copy these sentences. Fill in the missing words.

1 Anglo-Saxon villages often had a ____ to keep out wild animals.

2 The village leader was called the ____ .

3 Feasts were held in the thane's ____ .

4 Most Anglo-Saxon churches were made of ____ .

B Write a sentence to answer each question.

1 How did many Anglo-Saxons arrange their villages?

2 What did the women wear?

3 How do we know that the Anglo-Saxons used stone?

4 Why do you think only a small number of Anglo-Saxon churches can be seen today?

VOCABULARY

Days and months

Look
Cover
Remember
Write
Check

Anglo-Saxons believed in many gods; each had a different power and was worshipped on a different day. Tiw was the god of war and he was remembered on Tuesdays. Thursday was the day to worship Thor, the god of thunder. The most powerful god was Woden and his wife was called Freya.

Sunday	Thursday
Monday	Friday
Tuesday	Saturday
Wednesday	

January	May	September
February	June	October
March	July	November
April	August	December

A Copy these sentences. Fill in the missing words.

1 ____ is the day Tiw was worshipped.

2 Woden was worshipped on ____ .

3 Friday was ____ 's special day.

4 ____ is the first month, named after the god Janus.

5 ____ comes between July and September.

6 What are Sunday and Monday named after?

Remember, nouns are sometimes called 'naming' words.

A **noun** is the name of something.

A **proper noun** is the *special* name of a person, a group of people, or a place. The names of days and months are also proper nouns.

Proper nouns always begin with a capital letter.
Examples: Mary Sheffield Friday July Anglo-Saxon

A Write out the proper nouns in these lists.

1 women Tiw Thor gods Woden

2 Wednesday today Sunday day Tuesday

3 month August week April May

4 boy Susan Hamish girl sister

5 town Glasgow Belfast city Swansea

6 India country land France sea

B Write these sentences. Make sure you start with a capital letter and end with a full stop. Give each proper noun a capital letter.

1 the most powerful god was woden

2 thor was worshipped on thursdays

3 alfred was an anglo-saxon king

4 the anglo-saxons stayed mainly in england and did not invade scotland, wales or ireland

thistle

There are many words which have the **th** pattern.
Here are some of them.

the	thane	clothes	teeth
they	Thor	father	tooth
there	Thursday	without	moth
these	three	other	north
then	thick	mother	south
them	thaw	another	path
their	thistle	brother	bath

A Copy these sentences. Fill in the missing letters.
The words above will help you.

1 The th____ is the flower of Scotland.

2 An Anglo-Saxon village leader was called a th____.

3 Anglo-Saxon __th__ were often made of wool.

4 Th____ was an Anglo-Saxon god.

5 A ____th is a flying insect.

B Copy three words from each list.
Learn them, and ask a friend to test you.

Look
Cover
Remember
Write
Check

QUIZ

Letter squares

Make as many words as you can using the letters in the
square. Every word must have **th** in it somewhere.

t	y	w	e
r		**th**	n
o			m
s	e	i	a

Check-up 2

A Use **was** or **were** to finish these sentences.

1 It ＿＿ a cold night.

2 The rain ＿＿ falling.

3 The boys ＿＿ getting very wet.

4 Owls ＿＿ hooting and screeching.

5 They ＿＿ very pleased to get home.

B It's a cold and miserable night. The boys hear a distant rumble of thunder. The wind is whistling through the trees. Owls hoot and screech nearby. Leaves crunch and twigs crack under their feet. "I don't like it here, we shouldn't have come," says Carl. "I'm scared," agrees Tim. They'll be pleased to be home.

1 Write the onomatopoeic words (sound words) in this passage.

2 Think of two other onomatopoeic words and put them in a sentence.

C Write the five contractions in the passage.
Next to each write the other way it could be written.
The first is done to help you.

1 It's = It is

46

D These definitions are jumbled. Write them out correctly.

home	the season between Summer and Winter
wind	a deep, low noise
Autumn	where we live
protect	a device for keeping the rain off
rumble	moving air
umbrella	keep safe

E Copy the headings below.

types of tree   **weather**   **grow on trees**

Put these words under the correct heading.

nuts   beech   wind   berries   pine   hail
snow   blossom   oak   rain   leaves   ash

F Write one word to answer these questions.

1 Which is the first month of the year?

2 Which is the last month of the year?

3 Which is the month before March?

4 Which day comes after Wednesday?

5 Which day comes between Friday and Sunday?

GRAMMAR AND PUNCTUATION

A Adjectives are the words we use to describe things. Write down the adjectives in each sentence.

1 The little girl threw the red ball.

2 Big waves crashed on the sandy beach.

3 The hot sun melted our cold ice-creams.

B Look at the sentences again.

1 Write a list of the verbs ('active' words).

2 Write a list of the nouns ('naming' words).

47

C In these sentences the punctuation has been left out. Put in the missing capital letters, full stops and question marks.

1 i like going on holiday

2 jenny and liam played on the beach

3 do you want to go for a swim

4 when will uncle sajid be here

D Conjunctions are small 'joining' words. Use **and** or **but** to join these short sentences. You may want to change one or two words to make the new sentence easier to read.

1 I like toffee-apples. Gill does not like toffee-apples.

2 Jackie went to see the Punch and Judy show. Tracey wanted to do something more exciting.

3 Ben's costume is red. Darren's costume is red.

E Every English word has a vowel letter or a letter **y**. Copy these words and draw a neat circle round the vowels.

hat	mug	glass	costume
bucket	spade	beach	sky

F Write these sentences. Put in the missing commas.

1 Mum brought sandwiches fruit biscuits crisps and drinks.

2 We carried the towels ball chairs picnic bucket and spades.

3 We did lots of things like swimming digging running jumping and paddling.

G Write down the proper nouns in these lists.

1 boy Dan Kim girl Peter

2 town London village city Birmingham

3 Wales country Yorkshire Antrim county